PIVOT

PIVOT

poems by

Debbie Richard

illustrated by Ashley Teets

Adelaide Books
New York / Lisbon
2019

PIVOT
a collection of poems by
Debbie Richard
illustrated by Ashley Teets

Copyright © 2019 by Debbie Richard
Cover design by Ashley Teets

Published by Adelaide Books, New York / Lisbon
adelaidebooks.org

Editor-in-Chief
Stevan V. Nikolic

For any information, please address Adelaide Books
at info@adelaidebooks.org
or write to:
Adelaide Books
244 Fifth Ave. Suite D27
New York, NY, 10001

ISBN13: 978-1-949180-72-5
ISBN10: 1-949180-72-7

Printed in the United States of America

Dedicated
to the memory of my parents,
Naomi Karen Richard and Arlis Dewain Richard

and Ashley Teets,
whose beautiful illustrations brought my poetry to life.

Contents

Landing It

When the skater takes the ice,
the crowd erupts,
the whole arena bursts into applause,
and sits mesmerized for nearly three minutes
of jumps, spins, and footwork –
an Olympian-hopeful's
concentration and reserve
 released –
as she lands the final jump,
skates cutting into ice,
unleashing a spray of crystals
as flowers shower the arena floor.

Changed

I've seen a brilliant light, an illumination
    of my soul – dark, ugly, violent.
Blind, as though a veil were drawn,
    casting shadows,
        hindering the fervor
            of my veritable quest.

I've been feared, resented, rejected
    by fellowman,
        beast, and disciple.
Despite all this, I am a chosen vessel
    to herald His name before men,
        to encourage,
            to exhort,
                to bring hope.
A change has taken place.
    The love of the Father
        has been bestowed upon me.
            I see a *new* path before me.
                I am Saul.

Clandestine Assignment

I carried the black pouch of diamonds
inside my London Fog. My heels made
a sharp, cutting sound on the pavement
as I darted inside an alley, just in time
to avoid the headlights from a patrol car.
I continued to the wharf, glancing over
my shoulder to see if I'd been followed.
I'd done this a dozen times before, yet
the adrenaline rush was still high.
My breath came in short gasps, my hands
were stuffed inside my pockets, lest their
shaking deterred me from my assignment.
Just as a figure stepped out of the shadows,
walking towards me with a determined gait,
I suppressed the scream rising in my throat.
The shiny object, which he pulled from his
coat, was pointed directly at me; A shot at
such short range would be fatal.
Then I awoke, with sweat on my brow,
And fell back on my pillows.

Perennial

When she died, I thought her flowers would die with her
For I was never the one with a green thumb.

Donning floral work gloves, brushing aside dead leaves
And old pine straw from the year before,
She loved digging in the dirt, cleaning out the flower bed,
Hauling rich soil in the bright red wheelbarrow,
Planting new seeds and bulbs,
Watching life spring forth from the earth.

The Shasta Daisies, white with a yellow center,
Perhaps the tallest ever this year,
Their sprightly heads tossing in the breeze;
The royal purple Iris, growing in clusters
Near the side of the house;
The English Rose, courtly –
Passed down through generations;
The splendor of the fuchsia Hibiscus
And multicolored Lantana are well on their way.

Though her body lies still beneath the earth,
Her spirit lives on, perpetual, never-ending,
Like the perennials whose roots remain alive,
Just waiting for the earth to burst forth
and beauty returns.

Closing In

Caught in the downpour,
my umbrella turned upward
like a teacup in the wind,
I hurry inside the cottage,
my green and white checked
dress shrinking steadily,
closing in on me–
giving a new meaning to
this fabric, *seersucker*.

Tickling Your Senses

This morning, I parked my car at the public beach access,
unloaded my beach chair and beach bag, then headed down
the sandy path towards the ocean, past the palms
and deep orange flowers that grow almost anywhere
in sandy soil. The sky was blue with billowy white clouds
and seagulls squawking overhead. The salt air was
mingled with the scent of tropical coconut oil.
Vacationers and locals occupied space quickly with
their bright colored umbrellas, beach chairs, and coolers.
A volleyball game with an imaginary net was underway.
Depositing my beach gear in the sand, I grabbed my camera
and headed down to the water's edge in time to snap pictures
of boats passing by. I looked down at the water as the tide
washed in, catching a glimpse of a large crab trying to bury
itself in the sand, its legs flailing frantically like changing
gears on some large piece of machinery; It had no worries
from me; I wasn't getting close enough to get my toes pinched.

The Answer

The lovely woman, impeccably dressed,
slipped into the backseat of the waiting car,
closed the door and sat quietly as the driver
pulled away from the clinic. Glancing in the
rearview mirror, he noticed tears streaming
down her cheeks, spilling onto her pink wool
sweater. As their eyes met in the mirror,
she shook her head, the answer resounding
between them louder than if she'd spoken.
She looked out the window, observing more
on this fateful day than on any other visit.

17

Between Two Worlds

Sitting in the lobby of the attorney's office this morning, I drank in the rich mahogany tones of the wood molding shaping this room, the burgundy and hunter green theme from the high-back upholstered chairs with someone's family crest design, to the matting in the paintings on the wall, framed in rich gold and brass hues portraying attorneys from long ago in their period attire, pouring over legal documents.

The blades of the ceiling fan, just above the small glass chandelier enclosed in a square gold gilded cage, were of the same mahogany tones. The shiny, lacquer finish of the bowfront chest of drawers against one wall appeared to be of an exotic design.

I was there to seek legal counsel, agonizing over selling the home my mother and I had shared for many years. Memories remain in that house - sometimes overwhelming, picturing her struggling with her walker from room to room, yet so independent, strong as the deep tones in that anteroom this morning.

Don't grieve for me, she whispered, nearing the end of her life, wishing me happiness – yet knowing how difficult that would be without her. Would this legal counsel be able to still my fears, the apprehension of releasing the only familiar thing I had left?

To break free – start a new life, one worth living.

The Abandoned House

The old gray house, void of doors or windows,
stood desolate at the base of the hollow,
a gateway to what lie ahead in the woods.
The house itself held an unusual appeal to two young girls
who pictured themselves as another Nancy Drew.
Our imagination running wild, we began to picture
what might have taken place here.
Mystery sleuths as we were, we wrote notes on scraps
of paper we found in our pockets,
and tucked them in a crack in the wall – a safe place
until we returned – or so we thought.
Little did we know that the local Boy Scout troop
was planning a campout that weekend, and the old house
would be a refuge from the coming storm.
The boys found the notes – much to their amusement –
and to our dismay, I might add – as I found out
the next morning when my brother brought them by our
house for hot chocolate.
I hid myself in my upstairs bedroom until I was sure
all the troops had retreated.

The Whippoorwill

As I lie awake on a late summer's eve,
The moonlight streams through my window panes,
The familiar call through the night rings out,
The whippoorwill calls to his mate again.

By day, he sleeps on the forest floor,
And is rarely seen by the human eye,
His wings blend in with the dying leaves,
But at night comes the familiar cry…
"Whip-poor-will, Whip-poor-will,
Whip-poor-will"

Unrestrained

A fishing pier was in the distance with a gazebo at the far end.
I've been on that pier several times before, walked out

to the very end, where there was nothing on the horizon
but sea and sky – an awesome sight. If I'd climbed up

on the rail at the end of the pier, which is shaped like
the bow of a ship, threw my arms out in sweet abandon,

tilted my head back, letting the sea breeze whip my hair,
perhaps I'd feel like Rose on that *unsinkable* ship.

A Single Rose

A single rose you picked for me,
And brought it to my side,
For I was ill, and upon my couch,
At dusk, at eventide.

This gesture spoke much louder,
Than first it would appear,
So precious was each rose to you,
For soon, they'd disappear.

The River

The nine-year-old walked along the river bank
with her friend, talking about nothing in

particular, and everything at once. As her foot
slipped, she rolled over the hill and into the deep

water, disappearing and then emerging again –
as her little friend stood mesmerized with fear.

Bobbing up and down, gasping for air, she
yelled for help. Her friend vaulted from her

paralyzed state and ran towards the campsite,
screaming. The father ran in the direction of the screams,

adrenalin kicking in. Sliding down the river bank,
catching himself on tree roots and weeds as he

approached the water, he dived in after her. They
emerged soaked, but alive. He delivered her little

shaking body to her mother who was now standing
at the top of the river bank, riveted with fear.

Flawless
(for Jay)

Traveling all night with a reluctant driver,
you jeopardized your own health to see our mother
when she was nearing the end of her life.

Sensing this would be the last time you would
see her alive, you knew you had to get there,
at any cost.

Never having the opportunity to work a public job
or drive a vehicle on public highways was much harder
for you not to do those things, than to do them.

You were her youngest child, born with an impaired heart.
Our mother spent countless hours at your bedside when you
were only seven and had your first open-heart surgery.

Now, you felt an urgency to be at her bedside, to be
in her presence, a connection so strong
as if the umbilical cord had not been severed.

Doctors implanted a pacemaker to regulate your heartbeat,
but when it comes to the affections of the heart,
yours has a flawless rhythm.

What can be implanted in those whose hearts are as fortified
as stone, cold, unfeeling? You have a kind, gentle spirit,
and a genuine concern for others - hardly subnormal.

How could a defective heart hold so much love?

24

Chasm

We gaze at each other across the courtroom,
You on the witness stand,
Me in the front row, waiting.
A deep chasm between us now,
Where once we held each other close.

The judge asks if there's any chance of reconciliation,
You answer quietly, "I don't think so."
Yet, you filed the papers; You left to "find yourself."
How could you answer, "I don't think so?"
Don't you know?

A Place

There's a place in the country
where a little white church once stood.

It had a single front door and three windows
on either side of the building. It's gone now.

An open field is there. Weeds have grown
where the building stood, as a beacon in that

rural community. Now, an occasional bramble
winds its way around a fence post.

My mother remembers when she
played the upright piano there as a girl.

She often walked to church with her
brothers and sisters and her mother;

her father, too, when he was not
working away from home.

Later, the preacher would come home
with them to share Sunday dinner.

The men and boys sat on the front porch,
watched the cars go by – occasionally

threw up a hand in greeting. A small
community; practically everyone was friend

or neighbor. The girls busied themselves
in the kitchen, helping their mother get

dinner on the table for their honored guest.
Nothing fancy – fried chicken, mashed

potatoes, green beans from the garden,
hot biscuits, and cobbler for dessert.

From the way my mother lovingly
describes this place, I often go there.

A place, in my mind.

For Now

The bills are poured out across
the kitchen table like a deck of cards.

The calculator is quiet now, the
only sound is the steady tapping

of a pencil. The half cup of coffee
has gotten cold, as I agonize over

where the money will come from. What
choice do I have? I've mulled it over

in my mind a hundred times or more.
I take down my straw hat from the brown

peg on the wall, and slip my feet into
the black boots by the door. Sloshing

through the mud to the barn, pail in hand,
I hear Cherry's bawl, protesting the hour;

I'm late this morning. For now, I'll take
pleasure in the quiet – just before the children

come bounding down the stairs – their smiles
as bright as the sun which peeks through the

barn door; No worry on their young brows.
The bills? I'll think about that tomorrow.

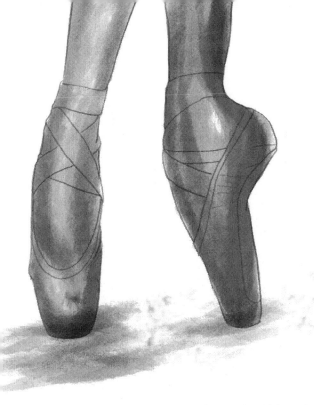

Lissome

She watched her daughter
waltz onto the stage
in her silver-tinseled angel wings,
white flowing gown and satin slippers,
laced and tied around the ankles.
The angelic being arched her back,
arms swaying gracefully
as she glides across the floor,
becoming one with the music,
feather-light,
whirling harmoniously,
and then –
teetering on trembling toes,
as the crescendo subsides.

Anything but a Hireling

(for Pastor Turner)

As one who shepherds the flock, you are not as the mercenary
Philistines, eager
with selfish desires, but one who has an attendant spirit, wisely
obeying its signals.

Your calling comes from a divine source, not regulated by man
or his time clock,
and when danger lurks or sickness infects, you are a constant
companion and guide.

Accompanying us through joys and disappointments, failures
and triumphs, you
are not unaffected by our feelings of humiliation, distress
or delight.

Surrendering your family time, something so precious, to minister
to our families,
becomes holy in an accepted sacrifice between the human and
the divine.

Air Maneuvers

You dove between your two companions,
Twirling, you floated on your back,
Your underbelly pointed toward the sun,
Your wings, grey, outstretched for balance,
Free as the breeze which carried you
Through these maneuvers.

Recruiting another, and yet another
Until your troops were eight,
You dove again, almost landing,
The gear poised, sure as an acrobat's footing,
Minus the tight rope or safety net.

Manipulating the flight path
Through a change of positions,
You mesmerized the crowd below
As if this were a military exercise.

In a shift of tactics, you steered the forces
En route further down the beach
To carry out yet another performance.
Who would have thought seagulls were so clever?

Mama's Corsages

Today, while doing a menial chore, cleaning out the refrigerator –
I found two wrist corsages - just alike - miniature white roses,
Tied with a white satin ribbon, the ones Mama received at church
On "Honoring Widows" Sunday – those past two years...

Nestled in clear plastic containers, in the bottom of the refrigerator,
Way in the back, on either side of the box of Arm & Hammer baking soda
That needed replacing ages ago. Corsages tucked away for preserving,
Just as a Christmas cactus might be tucked away in a cellar or cool basement.

Dumping old jars of relishes and jellies, some sprouting viridian colors,
Some, there since before mama died. The horseradish sauce I bought her,
The kind she liked to put on a sandwich, to give it that extra little "bite,"
The tall plastic container of cayenne pepper, outdated two years ago,
The jar of Green Tomato Pepper Butter we had canned together.

How I miss those days, working together in the kitchen,
Mama and daughter, side by side.
She took such pleasure in sharing with others –
Mama enjoyed seeing someone's eyes light up when she gave them
Some of her homemade sourdough rolls or honey wheat bread.

I'm not sure why I've held on to all of these things,
Things I knew were of no real value.
Yet, somehow having them near me meant she wasn't really gone.
Today, I threw away the outdated bottles and jars,
Yet, tucked the two plastic containers back in the bottom of the refrigerator,
One on either side of the baking soda,
Just where she would have wanted them to stay.

White corsages - cool, distant, preserved.
Just like the cellar cactus – tucked away, safe for another day,
When I need to remember.

Played Out
(for Loran)

We came and we came
And we took and we took
And you gave and you gave.
You listened as we shared
Our grief and our loss
While your own grief
Tore at your insides like a cancer.
Your own pain pierced like a Roman's sword.
Your own loss was resurrected time and again
Until you had nothing left.
Week after week, day after day,
We drained you like the last slurp of soda through a straw,
Like the last drop of ink in a well.
You were beaten, played out –
Until your body cried, "No More!"

Shell Island

Embarking on a day's adventure
to Shell Island, I glance back
from our shuttle boat as we
leave the dock. Passing lighthouses,

shrimp boats and familiar Georgetown,
we arrive safely. The captain pulls
away, leaving us to our treasures.
Combing the beach, past windswept

dunes, stepping over gnarled
driftwood that has washed ashore,
looking at our treasures – shells
that we will display in baskets or jars –

we nearly trip over something, a small
shark, deposited on this unspoiled
island, as desolate as the life
that was taken from him.

In the Garden

Flowers surround us –
　　　　tall green plants loom over tables,
Varied colors of gladiolus in white baskets
　　　　line the walkway,
The wicker basket from the doctor and staff
　　　　sit by the TV.

The funeral is over, and these are meant to
　　　　comfort us?
The smell of death surrounds us. How can
　　　　we separate the two?
We take them outside and dispose
　　　　of them in the garden.

I Close My Eyes To See…

  the wind chimes on the veranda
as they rattle in the breeze,

  the bumblebee swarming around the
rosebush and across the front porch,

  the fire truck's siren screaming as
it leaves the station,

  the loud speaker at school –
blaring out morning announcements,

  the band playing at half-time at a Friday
night football game,

  the leaves rustling on the trees
just before a storm.

Pilferer

A raven sat upon a rail,
and what fair things saw he?
A seagull flying overhead,
a deep and shining sea.

He looked upon the passers-by,
he gazed at one and all,
And marveled at the young, the old,
the short ones and the tall.

The sights and sounds of lapping waves
upon the shore so near
Could only add to wonderment
along this fishing pier.

By chance, if he could be so swift –
a fisherman's eye to tease,
Hence, his dinner would he catch,
with momentary ease.

Wildlife Center

The shaded path
curves through woods,
as we view
the black bear, coyote,
and mountain lion
in their natural habitat.
Otters exhibit their amazing
swimming abilities both above
and below the surface,
while the elk and bison
roam freely
over acres of land,
giving a realistic view
of wildlife,
almost as free
as the Creator's design.

Pendulum

You call on behalf of...
   Special Olympics,
      Retired policemen, or
         Campaign endorsements...
Your annoying calls
   come on Sundays
      or evenings
         when you think I'll be home.

Who is going to endorse me?
I'm full-time caregiver for my mother.
Do you want to contribute to *my* cause?
Clunk! Goes the phone.

I'd like to climb to the top of a Ferris Wheel,
   Clasp my palms around the cold metal frame
      Until my knuckles turn white,
         and hang suspended in mid-air,
           as free as a pendulum,
      Swaying back and forth,
     With the wind blowing through my hair.

Follow Through

(For Dr. T. Chuck Mills)

I wrote a poem for you once, presented it to you as proud
as a child presenting a "masterpiece" to her parents,
coloring inside the lines for the first time.

I was about as seasoned as a child, then, in the craft of writing,
composing only in rhyme. At least the sentiment was there,
the feeling was there.

I told you what you had done for me as if you hadn't realized.
I was writing the prescription myself. I envisioned a long journey
before me, with you along as guide.

Looking back, I had no idea then what we would face together.
I brought my mother to see you often. First, walking in by herself,
then with the help of a cane to pushing her walker with the wheels
and fancy seat, and finally in the chair, which I wheeled for her.

You had seen her as a vibrant, independent woman, as I had.
But over time... Time – that measurable period which an action,
process or condition exists or continues. How fitting a description.

We watched together as her vitality dwindled. Events succeeded
one another from past through present to future. Yet, you were
there to give her a hug, a word of encouragement. Thank you
for making her smile, and for helping her complete her journey.

Harmony

I recognize your footsteps in the hallway,
among so many others. My breath catches
as I sense your nearness, even though
I haven't seen you yet. The soft touch
of your hand upon my shoulder
sends pulsations through every nerve ending
of my body like static electricity to a wool sweater.
Your fingers running up and down my spine
are as familiar as ivory keys to a pianist;
a concerto only I can hear, only I can feel.
We sense everything so deeply, you and I.
The poetry we compose ourselves
and read aloud to each other,
the music we listen to – classical, operatic.
I want to step onto an empty dance floor,
with no one else there but you and I,
and I want to hear the music and dance.
I want to float across the stage
as you take me in your arms,
the passion in your eyes transfused into mine.
How could we not belong together,
we're already one.

Day at the Beach

Multicolored chute soaring o'er the waves,
Wind directed, yet anchored.
Children frolic along the shore
With sand buckets and shovels,
Knightly castles under construction.

The wind shifts, and we nearly kiss the crest,
A sudden stir, and we're drawn up again,
Free as a waterfowl –
All cares and worries lost,
In the froth, beneath our parasail.

Grandmother's Vines

It was still daylight
on those end-of-summer evenings
when we, as children,
were put to bed early,
though it was still light outside
and grandmother
was in her garden, working.
The cow milked, the chickens fed,
and the supper dishes washed and put away.
Now, at day's end,
she turns to her garden,
a place of quietude,
where alone, in tranquility
she plucks the legumes,
the rest of her day complete.
All that remains –
     the pungent smell of bean vines.

Lifeline

I was born Appalachian. Branded – *illiterate, mountain feuding, barefoot hillbilly.* Some would run from the hollows, elope if need be to escape this stereotype, ashamed of their heritage.

We went barefoot in summer, not from necessity, but because we loved the feel of the cool water from wading the creek and the dirt roads beneath our feet. The woods would often be ablaze with color as though reflected from an autumn bonfire. The road was shaded and cool, the dirt had been packed down so tight from years of travel, you could almost skip a rock across it. I'd smack my foot down hard on that cool ground like a toddler proud of his first march through a mud puddle.

Our education started out in a two-room schoolhouse where we played hopscotch on the covered cement porch, but life was the best teacher. Grandma took us to Sunday school at the little white Methodist Church where Sue played the upright piano, and we stood to sing the songs of Zion, being careful not to get pinched by those dark, pallet-style wooden pews.

Times were rough, and we knew all about sacrifice. Grandma watched her two-story house go up in flames just weeks before her daughter was to be born, and felt the loss of dividing up the other children among families in that rural community.

Dad worked in the oil fields, pumped wells, cut the locations with a mowing scythe, farmed, butchered hogs – whatever it took to feed the family. We washed clothes in the washing machine on the back porch where the ringer caught a pretty girl by the hair every once in awhile.

My parents cut down trees from over the ridge to build footbridges when the floods came and washed ours out. To keep out the chill in winter, colorful quilts and comforters were fashioned from scraps of material or clothes we had outgrown.

Later, some moved away from the hills, went to work in the city, and some even started their own business. As an adult, I moved further south to be near the ocean, but does that mean we are no longer Appalachian because we change our geographical location? My roots are deep in the hills of West Virginia, my lifeblood flows from the veins of those mountain folk who taught us survival skills, whose memories I will forever hold invaluable.

A connection I'm proud to call my *heritage.*

The Cellar

Wide, wooden shelves line three walls as I step
Barefoot onto the cool cement floor of the cellar –
Half hidden, half concealed by the earth's recess,
A welcome retreat on a sultry day.

A swift glance takes in mason jars, old bottles,
And blue-green glass insulators lining the shelves.
A single bulb with a long string, suspended from the ceiling
Is the only glimmer of light in this shelter.

Quart jars of bright red tomato juice, corn, pickles,
And the Half-runner green beans
Are arranged in neat rows.
Jellies, jams, and preserves are in smaller jars.

Bushels of potatoes are piled high in wooden bins,
The earth-scent still fresh upon them –
Sprinkled with a white powder-like substance called lime,
Used to preserve them from rotting through the winter.

Slabs of bacon and cured hams
Hang suspended from the tall ceiling
In the storage room, built above the cellar,
Another hideaway.

Meat, potatoes, vegetables.
All a body needs to survive another cold winter,
Carefully prepared and preserved –
A way of sustaining life in these hills.

Shattered

You promised to come, yet
I wait, poised, on this chair
as minutes tick by silently,
like a grandfather's clock
which has been broken —
also forgotten, discarded.

Those hands once moved,
as each sway of the pendulum
marked a promise
filled with hope.

Now, my hands are folded,
as still as the broken clock.
Can my heart be repaired?

In Memoriam

*(Dr. Clarence Maze, Jr., Former President of
Richard Bland College of the College of William & Mary)*

Your footsteps echo in the halls.
Pipe smoke wafts in from your study.

Students who traveled abroad with you and the *first lady*
undoubtedly cherish those memories.

Your niece and nephew fondly recall a colorfully
crafted purse and drum you brought them from Nigeria.

As a boy of West Virginia, you had an ingenious way of
getting things done, as in crafting your own sleds
for gliding over snow-capped hills.

You taught your sister – my mother – to play the piano
in the little white country church
where your family attended.

You hungered for an education and had the
tenacity to fulfill those dreams.

You instilled in your students
the assurance that their goals could also be achieved.

Your beautifully landscaped Water Garden
with its Japanese-style bridges, flowers, fountains, and waterfalls
continues to delight college students and the community.

Your contributions to the college,
as well as to your family and friends, were many.

Your ashes were buried;
Yet, your memory lives on.

Today we remember, and sigh.

To My Mother

I went to the sea
And the waves, sensing your presence,
Hurled against me.
I floated in the current
And reached for your hand
As I'd done so many times before.
I caught your gentle fingertips,
No – it was only a small piece of debris,
Soft, brown with short tentacles,
Churned up by the changing tide.
I looked skyward,
Felt the warmth on my face,
And knew you were there, somewhere.
I walked along the shore,
And picked up a shell, holding it to my ear,
To hear its message.
Instead of the ocean's roar,
I heard your whisper, *I miss you too.*
But, perhaps it was just the wind…

Separation

Screaming, kicking, yelling, your daughter came to us.
Only three months after our wedding – she was a teenager by then.
Walking on eggshells, I tried to be her friend.
Would we have had a chance if we had started out
As "two become one" instead of three in the marriage?
You said you would never lie to me, and you would always be there...
Where are you now?

The Visitor

The rust-colored butterfly, with black flecks on its wings,
lit on my mother's pink pants as she got out of the car.
I must be going to get a pair of pants that color,
she said, smiling, as she noticed the tiny visitor.
Turning to me, she remarked, *That's just an old saying.*
Though frail in body, her mind is still as sharp and witty
as the tiny butterfly is beautiful.

Prey

The gray and white gull
overhead
spread its wings,
then squawked
as it dove
to the water's edge.
Its long bill clasped
crabs and small fish
which the tide
surrendered to him.

Hinged

As a metal piece attaches a door or gate
Allowing it to open and close,
So are the memories of my childhood.

Some days I remember them joyfully, as if it were yesterday
When we explored the hills and hollows
And picked wildflowers or ventured down a new dirt road.

Other times, I find the door to my mind locked
As if a bank vault had closed for the night,
Dark, silent, no entrance.

Brandished

You raise your ugly head when I least expect you,
Tormenting my mind, disrupting those few hours
When sleep comes, intermittently –
Then, washing over me as a wave in an angry sea,
I gasp for air, while rough grains of sand
Tear at my flesh,
Like grinding salt into a raw wound,
Leaving me hollow, worn, grief-stricken.

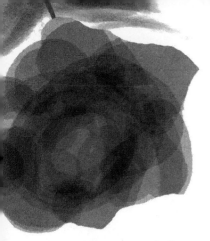

Resemblant

If I wrote a book about my dreams,
I wonder how it would be illustrated.
Would it unfold as a rose
with each delicate petal exposed,
unprotected, as a new chapter
in my life, for others to view.
Would it peak in beauty, or be hidden
inside the bud, tucked away
in that secret place,
shielded from injury –
the path I might have taken,
had I told you my true feelings,
both connate in nature.

Age of Innocence

This little girl, almost nine now,
plays with the simplicity of a child,
her toys scattered across the living room floor,
a favorite stuffed animal – a dolphin, gray
and white, lies abandoned now.

Sensing the need for comfort,
she climbs into her mother's lap,
reaches up to caress her cheek,
then snuggles in the curve of her arm
as sleep comes quietly to them both.

One so young, yet much older –
in feline years.

Luminescence

Exuding brilliance, you step into a room
as an actor steps onto a stage,
heads turn, instantly drawn to your smile,
the tilt of your head, the graceful
way you carry yourself –
an illumination of something deeper,
a mirror into your soul, the evidence
of the abode of something divine.

Incessant

*("But the water that I shall give him
shall be in him a well of water
springing up into everlasting life."John 4:14b)*

Clear, crystal water gushes out
from the side of the hill –
cupping my hands, I drink
from this freshwater spring,
a place, most familiar.

I had covered the length of this
dirt road many times as a child,
and found the spring at the base
of the hollow, the cool water
was always there, welcoming
as if waiting on a dear friend.

It reminded me of another source,
one of divine provision, sustaining us,
if we'll only drink
from its endless supply.

Chivalry is Not Dead!

Sending flowers for no special occasion,
Cooking dinner when she's had a hard day,
Running a hot bath and lighting candles
     for her pleasure only,
Leaving notes for her to find, while you're away,

Opening doors for her, even when her hands are not full,
Tucking her hand, protectively, inside the curve of your arm,
Smiling at her across a crowded room
     full of strangers,
Asking for a "date," without causing alarm,

Faithful to high moral standards,
Honorably, you've developed an art,
For it's those little things that show her
     you love her,
And occupies the biggest part of her heart.

The Years between the Dashes

"In the end, it's not the years in your life that count,
It's the life in your years." ~Abraham Lincoln

It's not my birth date, or the date I departed,
     that I want most remembered,
It's my laugh – was it infectious,
Were my words kind, my motives pure,
Did you smile when you thought of me,
     whether in the next room, or miles away,
Was I tenderhearted – did you notice,
Do you remember how I loved my mother, desperately,
Did I cook a meal for you, or bake a cake for your birthday,
Has my writing moved you in some way,
     or brought about a good memory,
Did I pray for you when you had a heavy heart,
It's been asked, *"If you were accused of being*
a Christian, would there be enough evidence to convict?"

It was my life's legacy – did you notice?

Ode to Earl Hamner

Mountain ridges, blue, hazy, yet strong and resilient
stretched before us as we traversed the route
to Schuyler, Virginia – the birthplace of a man, beloved
by countless numbers around the world.

The museum, formerly the schoolhouse, brick clad
with a row of windows across the front, framed by
a white door at either end, housed a treasure trove
of memorabilia of the Hamner family,
as well as The Waltons, the beloved television series
created by this man whose high school graduation picture
still hangs on one of the hallowed walls.
The stage in the former gymnasium, draped
with heavy navy blue curtains,
proudly displays the initials for Schuyler Elementary School.
From the bedroom with a "Boatwright" banner
hanging on the wall, to the infamous
"Recipe Room," fans were enthralled with this collection.

A short walk from the museum, the tall white structure
of the Hamner home welcomed us with its long front porch.
I realized I was entering a special place, most sacred.
The living room, warm with upholstered furniture
and a piano at one end, to the upstairs bedrooms, one
with a writer's desk and a "Big Chief" writing tablet,
to the kitchen with the long picnic-style wooden table
and benches, and green depression glassware,
reminding us of a place where this family spent many hours
sharing much more than meals, sharing their lives –
their daily happenings, and what a joy this must have been
for the parents of these lively "thoroughbreds."

Attending The Homecoming that weekend in Lynchburg
with hundreds of other Waltons followers, excitement
and anticipation permeated the conference center as fans and cast
members, many in period costume, came together for an elaborate
family-style banquet in the hotel ballroom, lit by brilliant chandeliers.

The magic of that weekend continued as we viewed a screening
of the new Earl Hamner Storyteller film with its director and producers.
We continue to be in awe of this man whose writing has touched our lives
and moved us to tears and laughter, whose family values have brought
us hope, a man whose creativity will no doubt impact others for generations
to come, a man who is as strong as his beloved Blue Ridge Mountains,
yet gentle and moved to tears by the death of a spider in his film adaptation
of Charlotte's Web, a true southern gentleman, humble, and nurturing
of aspiring writers, a man who has brought us together, the reason
we are here in the first place.

Resilient

She who seemed heartless
Once cared too much –

So much so, that *"no"*
Was not in her vocabulary

Overwhelmed, she slowly began letting go
Others mistook this for negligence

But it was her journey back
To where she'd once been.

67

About the Author

Debbie Richard is listed in the Directory of Poets & Writers as both a poet and creative nonfiction writer. Her poem, "Between Two Worlds," was selected as Adelaide Voices Literary Award for Poetry FINALIST for 2018. Her poems have appeared in Torrid Literature Journal, Adelaide Literary Magazine, Scarlet Leaf Review, WestWard Quarterly, Halcyon Days, and others. A chapbook of poetry entitled "Resiliency," was published in 2012 by Finishing Line Press. "Hills of Home," a memoir about growing up in Appalachia, was released in 2014 by eLectio Publishing. Her current project, a full-length volume of poetry entitled "PIVOT," illustrated by the award-winning artist/illustrator, Ashley Teets, has been published by Adelaide Books of New York.
www.debbierichard.com

About the Illustrator

Award winning illustrator, **Ashley Teets,** specializes in children's art, illustration, graphic design, and mural work. She earned a B.F.A focusing on visual art with a minor in creative writing from Alderson-Broaddus College in 2012. After completing two semesters of graduate work at West Virginia University, she continued her graduate study through the Simmons College satellite graduate program at the Eric Carle Museum of Picture Book Art in Amherst, Massachusetts where she studied children's literature and illustration. She holds a Masters degree in Arts Administration through the University of Kentucky. She has illustrated multiple award winning children's books that include 14 Mom's Choice Awards, four Indie Book and an Indie Excellence Award, an International Book Award, a USA News Best Book Award, and four Creative Child Magazine Awards. For more information please visit https://ashleyteetsillustration.com/.

Acknowledgments

Grateful acknowledgment is made to the editors of the following publications in which these poems have appeared or are forthcoming:

"Shell Island" – *Nature Writing*
"For Now" – *Founder's Favourites*
"Chivalry is Not Dead!" – *Halcyon Days*
"Between Two Worlds" – *Adelaide Voices Anthology 2018* (Finalist in Poetry Contest)
"Changed" – *Parousia Magazine*
"Shattered" – *Night Garden Journal*
 "Luminescence" – *Adelaide Literary Magazine*
"To My Mother" – *Adelaide Literary Magazine*
"Day at the Beach" – *Adelaide Literary Magazine*
"Air Maneuvers" – *Scarlet Leaf Review*
"Resemblant" – *Scarlet Leaf Review*
"Crawdad" – *Mountain Ink 2016*
"Harmony" – *Torrid Literature Journal*
"Pilferer" – *WestWard Quarterly*
"Hinged" – *WestWard Quarterly*
"Ode to Earl Hamner" – *Nelson County Times*

"Grandmother's Vines" - *Halcyon*
"Unrestrained" - *Halcyon*
"Tickling Your Senses" – *The Storyteller*
"The Cellar" – *Halcyon*
"The Whippoorwill" – *WestWard Quarterly*
"Lifeline" – *The Storyteller*
"Perennial" – *The Shine Journal-The Light Left Behind*
"In Memoriam" – *The Shine Journal-The Light Left Behind*
"A Single Rose" –*WestWard Quarterly*
"Mama's Corsages" – *The Shine Journal-The Light Left Behind*
"A Place" – *Two Lane Livin' Magazine*
"The River" – *The Storyteller*

I am also deeply grateful to **Earl Hamner, Jr.**, the late bestselling author of Spencer's Mountain and creator of the 1970's hit TV show The Waltons, who has been an inspiration, friend, and mentor, whom I miss very much.

Praises for Pivot

"Debbie Richard, in her poems, poignantly observes the values and needs, the pains and joys, in the human and natural worlds. She meshes all with the spiritual, her appreciation showered with grace, honesty, and love, and, finally, acceptance of what she cannot change. I love her poems."

-**DAVID SELBY** has had a long, distinguished career on stage and in film and television. He is perhaps best known for his roles as Quentin Collins in "Dark Shadows" and Richard Channing in "Falcon Crest." He earned a Millennium Award for distinguished acting from the Shakespeare Theatre in Washington, DC. He is the author of My Mother's Autumn and Promises of Love.

"In PIVOT, Debbie Richard moves from reflection to vision as she opens her world to the reader. Her attention to detail enables us to see through her eyes, whether recalling the feel of walking barefoot on soil, the smell of mahogany and leather in a lawyer's office, or mourning the loss of a loved one. Indeed, we see her pivot in life. Richard's work is accessible and fluid, easy to follow, even for those who tend to be intimidated by poetry. She is a poet-story teller,

tinged by Southern roots. This volume has been tastefully enhanced with beautiful illustrations, which adds to the pleasure and flow of the book, which has been a captivating read."
~**SALLY ARANGO RENATA**, writer and folk-artist, has been published in a number of venues including six anthologies, is twice a Pushcart Prize nominee, and was named Poetry Fellow 2009-2010 by SC Arts Commission.

"Delicately written and illustrated, these short poems are truly gifts from the heart. Richard's deep love of family, friends, home and Nature shines here. In her careful words, she captures loss and betrayal as movingly as affection, pleasure and joy."
~**CYNTHIA HODELL DYER**, Poet and Songwriter; Past President of S.C. Writers Workshop; Founding Director, Long Bay Threshold Singers

"Debbie Richard explores the beauty and honesty of love, regret, loss and the feelings that come after all of it. There is a delicacy and maturity in her frankness."
~**CARRIE McCULLOUGH JENKINS**, freelance editor / publishing consultant

54026589R00050

Made in the USA
Columbia, SC
26 March 2019